T0029472

SEVEN NIGHTS WITH THE CHINESE ZODIAC

For my sister,
Zhihong Yin.
And for all sisters

SEVEN NIGHTS WITH THE CHINESE ZODIAC

ANNA YIN

2015 Black Moss Press

Library and Archives Canada Cataloguing in Publication

Yin, Anna, author
    Seven nights with the Chinese zodiac / Anna Yin.

Poems.
ISBN 978-0-88753-553-6 (paperback)

        I. Title.

PS8464.I5S49 2015   C811'.6   C2015-903882-0

Edited by Meghan Desjardins
Designed by Jay Rankin and Shannon McLaughlin

The Palm Poets Series is published by Black Moss Press at 2450 Byng Road, Windsor, Ontario N8W 3E8. Canada. Black Moss books are distributed in Canada and the U.S. by Fitzhenry & Whiteside. All orders should be directed there.
        Fitzhenry & Whiteside
        195 Allstate Parkway
        Markham, ON
        L3R 4T8

Black Moss would like to acknowledge the generous financial support from both the Canada Council for the Arts and the Ontario Arts Council.

ONTARIO ARTS COUNCIL
CONSEIL DES ARTS DE L'ONTARIO
an Ontario government agency
un organisme du gouvernement de l'Ontario

Canada Council   Conseil des arts
for the Arts   du Canada

Night Shades

*

moving with me
the winter landscape
and white shadow

*

outside the blue box
skeleton of praying mantis
the whole night rains

Seven Nights with the Chinese Zodiac

I

it isn't as in your other dream —
under a white bone-eyed moon
a green dragon quiet and tame;
you sleep with the Time Tower,
crowned by detached diamonds…

it is a winter season —
everywhere falls into *polar vortex* freeze
heavy icicles hang, flashing sunlight's glory…
an ice snake breathes cold and white

you long to rise and glow
body spiraling like a mountain road
tongue flicking —
                    dangerous and hot

II

a dark horse runs into your dream…

he stops and turns…
in the corner, a huge vase
stands by you

he sniffs the edge…
you remember you hid notes
there, gone with fire and wind

you plead
this is a ruined garden…
leave!

he lowers his head
licks your hands
nose pointing to the West…
he kicks his hooves

you open your eyes
moonlight pours in…

here you are, alone, for seasons
there he is, bare, in snow...
sunset gifts you a red gown —
        night takes it

III

you roam in hills...
enclosed by dandelion clocks

your shepherd calls to his circle game —
"make yourself blind..."

        blind

for years, you've followed the advice
for years, you've survived this blue planet

      ...

your finger tracing a forbidden city...
      clocks plucked out
    weightless wings
        carry seeds...

IV

the phoenix tree in the Summer Palace
no longer gathers its lush branches —
curling up under it is a white tiger

autumn fires burn over the enormous land
abundant fruit has been swept away

you stare at a white house...
white smoke lingers
among white-framed windows

9

the startled jade rabbit leaps...
a white moon looks back

V

the sky descends
the river rolls

in this closing-up world,
the dragon thunders behind hefty clouds
the earth quivers
the towers fall down

> Everywhere is the wild lament
> of lost souls.*

10

on the roof of a historic site
a rooster crows repeatedly:

> Don't be afraid.
> A boat will be provided.**

his crown becomes stunningly red

VI

into the huge vase, you fall —
on a looking glass
…shattered scales

pigs retreat into dark woods
oxes gaze at the broken window —
the rooster is dying with his throat cut

paparazzi rush in
cats chase them away

the dragon wears a giant mask
the tiger measures his own blood pressure

the police-monkey escorts a well-suited rat
followed by his cloned brothers
the rat makes a soft cough
his thin whiskers toss off a line
from a cartoon film:

 "All dreams are valid"

VII

the vase shakes…
a dark tree sprouts out

on its top, seven tulips
close one after another

you touch —
each tumbles like a snowflake…

the snake creeps in…
the vase cracks

     …broken

    r

     i

      b

    $

you wake up
a black river flows

12

*David Day, The Animals Within
**Margaret Atwood, "Another Visit to the Oracle"

Glass Ballet

A white swan
led by the moon's harp...
Its music waters down...
He praises her perfect dance.

She weeps
the night lake,
discerning Plath's dead fish
from a torn black swan —
her wings fiercely flapping
from the nightmare.

In his palm,
the crystal ball spins,
snowflakes fall...
exquisite like angels —
never thawing or breaking
in their glass grave.

13

The Unquiet Bed

after Dorothy Livesay (italicized line by
Sylvia Plath)

Shivering in storms,
our bed is a fragile boat.

Coldly you summon
an island, and you come to land.

I hear its cracking sound
I feel the water flooding in…

You do not do, you do not do.

The whole night, it echoes
the unquiet waves.

Goodnight

Once again I think of onions
while biting a golden apple.
Peeling its skin, I take pity on
its wasted smooth fibrous quality.
My heart needs warm supplement;
greetings from iPhones come and go,
yet all are ethereal tales.

Wish you health and happiness…
easily said but less weighty…
For this kind of lost moment, what I truly want
is to tell a few jokes and weep inside
like peeling another onion.

Distant street lamps, one by one,
blink off…
the solitary Still Life up high
is lonelier than a fruit plate.
Its gorgeous fresh colour among deep
shadows, I pace back and forth —
Goodnight, such a simple statement.
Yet the sun is hidden somewhere,
utterances of silence.

In Van Gogh's Gallery

From sunflowers and violets
to the wheat field and starry sky,
I pondered and listened.
I longed for the painter's brush
to dissect me into slices of the light spectrum,
hidden in the corner of a canvas — from where
I could watch visitors and myself
through different centuries,
with some kind of agreement,
each face's colour lost.

I heard a baby crying
from the depth of his sunflower.
I dared not touch the faint blue
vase, although the background
was lavish pink.
Under the stars, the church tower
cast shadows;
its chimes were choked by dark gravity.
I found myself standing in the center of the gallery.
Each painting seemed far
        far
away from me.

Apples and Pears

In addition to apples,
I have a special feeling toward pears.
I place them on the kitchen table,
but fear to pare them.
Soon they retreat to the wall of my living room.

Occasionally appearing in my dreams
at the same time are my dearest lover,
and the other, a stranger.
They are close, like the pair of pears
in the painting, shadows overlapped.

My hands slip in the moonlight,
the bittersweet fruit flavour
spreads in the cool night.

17

Caught

Can one tell
a labyrinth from a maze?

From a stormy life,
autumn gradually
lets go its flaming shades.

In a small city with a foreign accent,
you find yourself at an old station.

18

The wind is salty.
The train hasn't arrived.
The hall is hung with tapestries
in patterns of *Paradise Lost*.

You think of your lord
and the temple he built for you.
An oil lamp flickers in the corner.
Your suitcase remains heavy.

Over your head, the speaker
plays holiday music.
Your voucher drops.
You sigh. Someone
picks it up…

"Merci," you hear yourself say.
The train is hauling dreams…
You watch yourself get on and off.

Can one tell
a fog ahead from a solid wall?

19

Seven Dreams

1.
a growing watermelon
you carry under skin
through one arch to another

2.
first ultrasound
…heartbeats…
lullaby in dreams

3.
flooding and fire
out of nightmares
light startles at sleepless dawn

4.
mid-autumn moon…
your fists open…
counting butterflies

5.
balloon bursts
sirens all the way
your recurring dreams

6.
into the wilderness
a wolf stares, nights hollow
your empty belly

7.
among forget-me-not blues
candle-lit baby shoes
…starry night

Death

What is it like?
No one takes a close look.

When you were nine,
a road accident, a pool of blood.
You followed adults into a room...
all strangers, you touched the victim's foot,
wondering if it was the same coldness
as your grandma, who died in her sleep.

Nobody noticed you
or asked why you were there.
A curious kid, you were too young
to know the meaning of death
and to see the inaccessible walls of darkness.

Grown up, you dreamed of the dead
who appeared without faces...
What is death like? You wanted to ask,
but they just faded away.

Years later you started writing poetry —
the living ones come and go
all wearing veils,
visible or invisible.

Your pen is the skipping stones
falling into their rivers,
rippling outward
and asking
what life is like.

23

At Dante's House

At the end is the door.
It feels like eternity.
Last item is removed,
the knot looks newer.
Nothing indicates.
You hesitate — this
replays many times in your dream.

The moon is full, trees are thin.
A door leads to another,
the long hall yawns deep...
A doe steps in,
you wake up at the green.
You search for its italic code —
behind the curtain
an enormous foot looms.

"Why then do we not despair?"

after Anna Akhmatova

In a butterfly suit,
I hide my pessimistic skin.
Wrapping worries into a period,
I enter an oasis of oblivion.

My wings flutter effortlessly,
free…so called.

Travelers stop by, I offer —
the divine forgetfulness.
Shaking their heads, they race
for mirages of the gold finger.

I see evil's cloak sweeping the sky,
apparitions haunting behind…
I wish I could warn them
off cunning animal zones,
blind-minded battlefields,
clasping capital castles…

But my voice fades, my wings —
dead leaves — fall on ground.
The worries enclosed in my body
roll large and larger —
anytime to explode.

26

Fatality

I offer you fruit.
You only take a pomegranate.
Cutting it open,
I see the bleeding seeds.
You take twelve, swallow them
the same way your son swallows pills…

He goes into the Underworld,
no messages back and forth.
The whole year, you remain like a statue,
wearing the rest of the seeds.

I don't know
how to wake you up —
how to breach Hades' gates.

We wait for the seeds to dry out —
tickling red tears…red rivers…
then snow will cover
everything, everything,
even this story.

Dried Roses

*

dusting old books
hidden petals
with fading handwriting

*

slipping from fingers
the taste of winds
and morning dews

Late Trains

In our last call we talked about weather.
Spring is finally here and I forgave the long winter.
I intended not to mention those cold nights —
I moon-watered your poems.
They flowed into my veins, softening
my snow-buried garden...
No point to worry you,
I remarked that the wintersweet bloomed
...I could send you some shoots.

We two are orphans.
I remember a precious diary given to me
for my 18th birthday, so delicate and exquisite.
I wrote in it and saved it for you.
My handwriting still hasn't become better;
my best poems haven't arrived.
The diary grew out-of-date and eventually was
lost.

Our call ended with Mary Oliver's line,
poems are ropes to let down for the lost...

It is late here.
Below my window, night trains come and go.
I catch shadows of wings that only soar in dreams.

31

After So Long

with apologies to William Carlos Williams

I think I should write a love poem
before I forget how to love.
It will remind me of the scent,
the fire and the ocean.

A fine recipe is what I need,
not a stale sandwich from a lunch box
or the one at a fast food chain.
I open drawers to search
for seasons I recall.

32

But the bell will soon ring.
The door will swing open.
I could appear with a fox mask
and a box of iced plums.

A note you might find inside:
the night is coming,
the dinner is not ready;
the you and the me,
so sweet and so cold.

The Floating City

So many years, still you live in that city.
Your orchard has bloomed, blessed with fruits.
Your roots must have grown deep;
I've heard   you have been happy.

So many years, still I am the wandering
moon, far and away into other courses.
Some nights   I have dropped by
and watched a sad face in your mirror;

> *You might see or not —*
> *along with a long river.*

The fallen leaves, east winds picked up
and blown into you, now are in my mirror.
I guess I have my whispers there
and transcribe some to warm winter.

So many years, in my mirror
there are suns, rains
and the city you live in.
I might have forgotten many things;

I think winds do remember them.
When they are blown into my garden,
I cup each and think of

that night's moon, and the city that floats.

34

The Odyssey

We meet in your poems
where an open canal is built…
a hand-made canoe is provided.

I come alone —
with salty skin and panting voice.
Light is the anchor —
I call upon you.

A river rises in me…
Your veins deepen it.

Take me by line
breaks —
save me
when sirens
seduce.

35

Dear Reader

You ask,
"Do we believe love?"

I have waited for seasons…
The whole winter snows…
I ponder on how to utter "Yes."

I long to walk along your shore
to sparkle as summer's bonfire.

I want my eyes meeting yours,
my hands holding yours —
spreading seeds,
scooping heaven,
my feet becoming yours,
my breath exhaling yours…

The soil under us thaws,
the sky above us opens —
this is the garden.
We are the tree;
roots grow
together.

Here, Take Me

Not a strayed cat,
nor a hooked fish...

Roll up your sleeves,
strike a match...

I am on fire —
burning with scents...

Open your chamber...
Light up your tower...

I have come this far —
after sun beating down,
wind drying out,
pieces being cut
and wound up...

Now take me —
this pack of Paradise.

Valentine's Day

Flipping through a dictionary
I try to find its definition.
Stores all are filled with exaggerated
packages and exquisite celebrations.

Outside, an empty plastic bag
flies in the air, commuters look
indifferent.

Under the spotlight,
a print of a still life by Van Gogh
brought back from New York
comes alive,
I hear wineglasses clinking.

Spring is not too far
but I cannot find an address
to send the blossoms to,
neither anywhere to build a bridge
to an extended Paradise.

A Glass Onion

Well, John, you must understand
I was a little girl then…
Skipping stones on a soundless river,
I have missed ripples of the outer world.

Now your loyal fans fill me in…
They regret…the ruthless bullet took your life…
Yet looking through a glass onion,
everything is still there, your music, your love,
and *Hello, Goodbye…*

John, I have arrived —
through the *strawberry fields,*
upon the *bent-backed tulips*
into the *other half-lives…*
love me do, love me do…
the long and winding road
crosses the universe…

Yet thirty years have passed,
I open an enormous clam,
no pearl left, neither *Mr. Moonlight*.
I see *a fool on the hill*
trying to make a *dovetail* joint…

Looking through a glass onion,
everything is still there, your music, your love…
I cannot help but cry.

40

*all italicized words are lyrics by the Beatles

Edge Arts

The coffee table is round and black;
you put down your hot cup.
I wear my dark sunglasses,
a pink curving scarf wraps me
— a fish in the water tank.

We walk through the arches
of the Parliament building.
I stop to say goodbye;
you press lips on my cheeks.

In this snowy season,
the gift shop sells
moose droppings.
I watch my train turning
into a white wild horse.

The Sin City

Here, I could fall in love
with a splendid snake.
My plain soul longs for style
and fades into a rippling mirror.

It is fine to get lost
among enticements.
Everything wears infinite hues,
each speaks volumes of glamour.

In gleaming colours, the snake swallows the sky.
The tree from the Garden falls.

Will I stay or leave?
My skin is thinner,
I battle with the love of sin,
and become sinful.

The sun turns itself
        into a giant sizzling apple.

Lunch

I could wait
and ask for water
without ice

the whole afternoon
I could make excuses for you

and sketch a long story
of a goldfish
in my glass

1000x
fresh air
refilling water
how easily we survive

the roof wears a suspicious
cloud
I could blow it away
and preserve you
yes, the deep water

no shadow
no wave.

44

An Impossible Love

a conversation with Robbie Burns

"Be daring," you would plead,
"What is the harm in love?"

But this Anna isn't a red,
red rose that you might recall,
neither a white swan by summer lake.
Her heart is the loose string,
barely tied on any season.
Now it bleeds to its winter landscape,
exposed like the snowman.

Her eyes eat the sky,
her face is pastel paper.
So damn true, her love is
the sinking sand in deep blue.

45

Forget *Anna, Thy Charms*,
the love song with spent dreams…
the June melody and the warm sun
are high and higher — thousands
and thousands of miles
away — her white shadow
remains speechless.

46

Valentine's Colour

The first time, it is red,
the second time...pink
third...blue...
then black...

The same date,
the similar story.

The convenience store sells all kinds of hearts,
long-stem roses and numerous chocolates.
The owner prunes extra leaves.

Why do I still buy one,
and think of you?

The colour in my vase
is white, white like ice.
We fill the vase
with frozen lies.

Life Jars

*

after heavy snow
someone spreads bread
along the trail

*

more snow
the icy willow leaning
...*spring, spring*

Snow

for my sister

> *This is the winter garden. White on white.*
> *Bunches of snow like cherry on the bough.*
> *— And Once More Saw the Stars*
> *(Philip Stratford)*

It must be a miracle.
The doctor told us
you wouldn't make the snow season.
But this year, in our warm south
winter comes earlier.
We rush to get fur coats from closets.
We are both happy and worried —
no one can predict the weather
and the future any more.
In the news, somewhere where
there are never floods;
now it is under deep water.
When we were young,
we waited for snow eagerly.
Following you, I made snow
angels, mine always smaller.

Does it snow in heaven?
Nobody tells us.
Those who go before us, you say,
go to check
and save a place for us.

51

My Father's Temple

When my father rebuilt his house,
on each stair he carved
his and my mother's names.
My father is not a superstitious or rich man,
with all of us grown up and living far away,
his narrow tall four-floor building
rose with our criticisms of its waste.
My father rolled his eyeballs, broke his silence:
"Find your own floor and stay longer."
He winked at us,
"At least none would buy."

My father's wisdom was defeated by the city plan.
Officers came along with bulldozers and demanded
he leave.
My father climbed up to the roof, and refused to move.
Holding his camera, my father shot his last photo
in the knocked down neighbourhood.

I received a copy of the photo in the local newspaper.
My father looked so small on the top of the ruins.
It was titled, "The Last Temple."

Mistakes

There is a mirror that has seen me for the last time,
There is a door I have shut...
      — "Limits" (Jorge Luis Borges)

Someone from our childhood mistook me for you —
his apology blew me back to midnight.

Once close like the folded rice paper,
bearing the same family name and a white swan
dream,
we too thought we could be sisters.

But we grew apart.

You drifted away into a night lake —
with feathers blackened by dark lust,
with slim neck hooked by golden bait.

Your parents cursed you and shut their door
behind you; mine forbade our gathering.

53

Rumours traveled fast…
In the distant city I too believed
wherever you went, you left an open
Pandora's box, but I refused to imagine —
What comes next?

One summer, I returned.
My fantasy was still stuck in a match box
with a white horse-mounted prince;
yet I heard your weeping.

54

Your ghostly face alarmed me…
I slapped you hard; your shadow shook.
Dragging you to the hospital, all I felt was my
crushed ribs.
The doctor said "Five minutes later — no hope"
You looked away, indifferent.

What's left to say?
Well, you married your gangster lover —
the dread and deadly horse…
I've collected stones
in a box with Pegasus and hope.

10th Anniversary

I have searched for months
for a pink dress, my favourite.
It is someplace where
I have saved it for a future date.
But since then, it fails to appear in any suitcase
or closet, vanished like the melting snow.

This season, so much to say.
I have said little,
pretending I could wait
for that warm day or night.
This is a box of icy plums.
You know how they taste.

A House Is a Tree

When young, I was told
in the East there was a Life Tree,
rested on by numerous birds.

Now in my house,
each room is taken
and claimed in a distinctive voice.

The red cardinal lives at the top.
Hopping down, he picks
a fight madly.
Shocked, the house trembles.

The black crow
aging in her own shadow,
startled, echoes each sound.
I think I am the blue one,
clasping a shawl over my head;
I flash into rains.

There is no forest ahead,
no stars nor bridges.
I won't want to think of
the way back.
But in the end I wake up
with a bare tree and a baby bird
clinging to me.

I learn to measure
a floating roof…
scooping up mud
as well as twigs —
the way to nest…

57

The Collage

I ask Mr. Mansaram,
"Any story?"
"No. It just happened.
When a lady stood there, I took a photo…"

No story.
Yet this carved shadowy cow stares at me,
and the lady looks familiar.
I guess lately I have too many thoughts of my own
sister.
Last night I dreamt of her.

But no news is good news.
This April, I flew back.
With silk scarves I brought to her,
I soothed my sister:
"Wrap your head, you look even prettier!"

The lady inside the collage faces away from us,
shaded by her long red scarf.
Surely I bought the same for my sister.
Mr. Mansaram doesn't know our story.
He smiles:
"You could write any story if you like."

But no news is good news.
I fear to write any.

Which Plant Are We?

The therapist leaves us alone,
papers scattered
on the table. Suddenly
we become quiet.

I remember when I was a kid
I drew lots of dandelion clocks —
beneath the morning sun, they breathe
freely, ready to take a windy ride.

Now it is getting dark.
The sunset casts its last light
on my paper. No dandelions.
Their seeds might land somewhere barren.
No roses either. They would turn
dark and dry over time.

I've read a poem about cactus trees:
so striking and so enticing, but the desert,
the thirst and the thorns are too hard to bear.
I decide I prefer orchards.

In our backyard, there are pears and apples.
But they never grow sweet to eat,
worms and birds are always ahead of us.

I think I had better be a pine —
at least an ideal fence.
On my paper my pencil
circles and circles —
layers and layers
of a glass onion.

61

Messages

In your message,
you say you miss me —
this simple and quiet life.

Here, the sun just rises.
I take a long walk in the trail.
A red cardinal hops in front.
Often I run into rabbits, squirrels and ducks.
Today the cardinal leads my way —
A surprise.

To reply, I want to ask about your girls,
99 spent roses…were they sweetness or sorrow?
Do you still hold one for someone?
How does it taste to raise your sparkling glass?

My path is illumined by the moon —
the same moon walked with Basho
whose lonely journey ended
on the narrow northern road.
I long to tell you
how the banana leaves weigh in rains
and how my soaked face fades.

The day breaks.
The cardinal is gone.
I spread seeds on white sheets —
they breed their own roses.

63

The Hole Story

I came in to complain —
"Life is *a loaded gun*,*
a watchful eye isn't enough."
My therapist nodded and explained
"Like any teapot or pressure-cooker,
we all need holes."
She assured me I have plenty —
my poems are derived from them.

But lately one after another,
they rain like cats and dogs.
I worry I might die like an empty log,
rather than as an explosion.

My neighbour nods to me whenever I pass by,
yet our eyes never meet.
His door always closes…I wonder
about his three young kids…
I walk around and find
his air conditioner runs the whole year.
My therapist suggests, "That might be his hole."

My boss was single, working hard like a clock,
first arrived — the last to leave.
Once I brought an extra apple and gave it to him.
The next day, the apple remained intact.
Only when he went for heart surgery
did he remember my apple, but found that
heaven isn't a physician, no medicine is posthumous.*
Now I eat two and work out as well.

My nine-year-old nephew loses his ping pong games.
His father scolds him: "Be a man, don't cry!"
I recall my brother at the same age crying harder
       for his strayed cat.
I pat my nephew's shoulder and hand him some
tissues…
But for my brother,
       this poem and my therapy clinic's card.

*based on Emily Dickinson's Life XLVII

Bread

after Bruce Meyer's A Book of Bread

The spoiled kid takes it for granted,
biting it once, then throwing it away.
Being used to that, his parents walk away
to mend their other matters.

The well-suited man sits in a glass building,
busy on his report in a pair of glittering shoes.
His willful blindness is obvious —
when encountering the homeless down the street
or on World Alive news, he flips his pages.

The bread store below is crowded,
its delicious aroma pulls in passers-by.
Every Sunday, as traditional,
bread is passed along and shared.

Somewhere else
children in rags.
Yet crumbs drop here,
and Hunger Games play;
even birds don't wait.

Visiting New York

this endless snowstorm
the Statue of Liberty
lost in white blindness

*

on window-shopping
savouring the term of mirage
downtown Manhattan

*

New Year's firework blooms
upon the Big Apple city
lights up my dream, still

*

doves and me
along the quiet Long Island
snapshots at 6am

*

recalling a poem
his shadow and mine expand
on Brooklyn Bridge

The Way

after Rae Armantrout

So many planets,
why the Earth?

"I am here."

Neither have I imitated you
nor believed in God.

Flags on moon —
we chat over cell phones.

"The girl killed by lightning,
liked a black dress."

In a story
made of trees
you survive.

I wear a white gown
to shape
a found poem.

Real life emergencies
come "upon" "again"...

69

(MH730)

......
0 1 0 1 0...
the missing black box

*

alone at twilight
shadows of an empty nest
sparse twigs overlapped

*

70

stopping at a green bench
someone's name carved
in the stone beside

*

palm reading
a flying fish
a river covered with snow

From the Department of Philosophy to Drama

I find your office, closed, of course.
A yellow dust cover is glued on your door,
a business card attached,
and a blue timetable remains blank.
I check the next door. The office seems to belong
to a professor with two winged horses pulling
a chariot.
I have the urge to read her agenda
in reverse, like a film run backwards.
I recall how you hold up the looking glass —
in the suit of reasons and games.
Speaking of that, I have brought my new manuscript,
piles of handwriting. Calligraphic tadpoles
swim in my night river and a ripped net.
I must apologize —
accidently I knocked over a bottle of perfume,
and now its scent is everywhere, "Allure" —
according to its ad.
The hall is quiet and no one queries me.
At the exit, I pick up a magazine, "*Now*" — for free.
Inside, there are film reviews and new drama.

I flip through it —
the immediate needs at your campus:
nude bodies with calling numbers,
all so lustful, so convenient.

72

Absence

In your email, you mention the celebration —
dancing in glamour for the significant moment.
From this east coast of the Pacific Ocean,
again, my fingers tap the familiar word, "Nostalgia."

The autumn moon casts its lustre on my blue
passport —
its wings fly elsewhere:
my hands rise with a solemn oath —
the five-starred red flag flutters my leaping heart.

The returned friends exclaim the events
are grand, forever stunning.
Their mood is cheered up even though
the sky there is too grey.

No surprise.
I pretend that is the excuse.

...Absence...

Yet at that moment, I long to be there...
I won't worry about bad news —
the plunging stocks
the air pollution index
the soaring house prices
and the landless farmers...

Together   we applaud and applaud.

74

Against Romance?

A stranger sent his love stories and asked for
my opinion.
What can I say? These two cities, Paris and Rome —
I long to visit. But visit alone (…)
I have been there many times in my dreams, always
with company —
Yet the difference:
My companion without a face,
but not without a soul.

75

The Natural

The young mother boasts on her Facebook
she and her boy often have naked swims at night.
That is how they return to the natural.

Lately I have declined invitations from a friend
who owns a nice backyard and a tranquil pond.
I fear even with swimsuits, I would still feel
naked…
In my bathroom, my mirror is the right size,
modestly stunning.

We Chat

We greet, we thank,
and we say goodbye.
My anxiety about this shallow peace
struggles to find an entrance and an exit.
The moon seems a fond topic, of course,
but it is too aloof beyond this discussion.
We recall a song that sings
life and dreams are forever
on a river's opposite sides.

You sigh I am an angel; I fear not.
Angels are from heaven,
not the random results from Google,
too many and all kinds of:
Angelfish, Angel's Trumpet, Angel Eyes,
Computer Virus Angels and Fallen Angels...

It is a pity that the search engine
has omitted the Snow Angel.
Winter is here, we get used to making many —
just lying down and sliding limbs,
when getting up, we leave angels behind.

The twilight breaks through,
we will soon end our chatting.
A post on a stranger's blog states:
"Every girl was once an angel without tears.
When she met her beloved, she began to taste
tears."

The rose by my window sparkles
with dewdrops — I tell you
believe it or not, today is sunny.

78

Lorna's Cat

She calls you "Basho" —
a name blown from remote Japan
and outliving the lonely banana tree,
a name pioneering the Narrow Road to the Deep North
and lighting up seven continents for centuries.

She must believe
you possess nine lives
each watching out for red moons,
and searching for a heavenly ladder
where you can suddenly disappear
then return with a glowing halo.

On snowy days,
she watches you inking
your paws on the rice papers,
so much like water splashing
from the old pond.

On rainy nights,
she makes tea, red or green.
You climb up her tall bookshelf.

The moonlight pours down
on parchment blossoms;
you fetch a book of haiku.

upon touching…
foliage and raindrops —
soft and sweet

Dream in Glass

This dream is in glass
thin and transparent.

Light comes through
not bending like that in gothic buildings
or kaleidoscoped with mosaic magic.

Have you ever filled it
with red wine and blue blues?
This dream has no colour;
no one can tell its bygones.

I pump in air and my fingers
tip in waterdrops —
they blend into a light
and lighter bubble.

Come, take a breath
then enter…
You could lift the kernel
or break it all at once.

This dream is in glass.
It has an open ceiling —
my heart is waiting…

82

Night Waves

"Your lines are from Heaven…"
After typing goodnight,
you left this message.

The dawning sky, sleepless…
I envision a full moon from a crescent.
The window of your office must be wide open —
hot there, a long day to exhale…

I want to send something,
something to savour,
something to embrace,
something to make cool,
only to find a long line casting
over the shore,
wave upon wave…
inhaling.

Shadowlight

The autumn gusts feel warm
as if it's spring.
I walk alone and recall
last night by accident I cut my finger...
slowly, on the rice paper, red roses grew.

If there is a messenger,
we should know the shadow
of our youth isn't void —
I still wear warm colours;
although leaves withered,
the tree grows silent.

Once I chased fireflies for green light.
Now the blue twilight flickers near.
Tell me, sage, if the coming winter is a white tale.
I long for snowflakes in your words,
delicate and fine, melting on my tongue.

The night descends.
Upon my palm, a river flows.

The Painting in Your Backyard

Her face rises in my dream;
her lips sing a siren song.

In your backyard, I watch
her curving body blending into
the autumn landscape;
a huge fish eye stares.

Winds pick up leaves,
red and yellow…
a dialogue tangled…
with Fire and Ice.
Your brush spreads blue as the final touch.

What does it open up or close in?
A young deer steps into your yard,
sniffing the newly formed frost.

I remember our last conversation
was about weather.

Life Jars

When I was a child,
I was told
silence is like light,
having colours and faces.

Walking through the country in the dark,
I used to fill a glass jar with fireflies.
It became my green starry compass.
When I inhaled the silence,
I could hear quiet voices from living creatures,
each making music of its own life.

Now grown up,
every day's busy journey in this hectic city,
I thought our life jars must be full of mundane
trifles and noises;
Yet wandering into ravines in this urban landscape,
I can find the silence, silence and silence —
Where it opens a door like sunrays breaking
through.

Riding along the lakeshore,
I see sunset's serene reflection on the lake,
the Port Credit lighthouse topping its splendour.

A baby swan takes off…
I inhale the silence.

87

The Self-Completing Tree

*

the river of Life
we are flowing
with dreams

*

full load of laundry
our whirling days
dry in the winds

*

bloody moon
looking for Easter Bunny
the child in me

The Absolute World Towers

What are you holding?
I ponder at your footings.
Against your modern gestures,
I long to trace my ancestors' migrant setting,
the beginning of a world, the Yin and the Yang,
the myth of life...circling in
and out like a winged spiral...

"Come," the well-suited salesman invites,
his official smile guaranteeing my grand entry.
"When the morning sun casts its slanting light,
you will find Marilyn Monroe's golden
and curved figure lingering..."

"But how about at night?"
I worry, *whether,*
after the glory is gone, grounded in gloom,
the shadow of an aged woman also weeps.

"Well, young lady" —
An aged man emerges.
He winks at the puzzled salesman:
"No one can stop an hourglass…"

The sun is setting.
Stunned, I rush to ask,
"*What* (else) *is past, or passing, or to come?*"*
The sage disappears
among the silhouettes
of "Sold Out" signs.

William Butler Yeats, Sailing to Byzantium

Ways of Flying

You are tired of his
molding, over and over,
thrashing, nailing
into you.

More and more
the weather has been unpredictable
— this statue is on the edge.

The wings you gave up,
now you long to reach —

You wade in the river
and watch golden fish in flight.

Do not wake up to disturb…
Do not wake up to disturb…

At dawn,
you take off.

Hesitating

The night is only a sort of carbon paper,
Blueblack, with the much-poked periods of stars
— Sylvia Plath

Insomnia is a stopped clock pendulum.
This summer night, you do not recall your name.
Your eyes are full of thorns,
floating above a nameless river.

Whose sleeves scattered in the scrub?
Blue moonlight, spilled seasons.
Your hands hold a silver mirror,
a long reflection.

A copper coin bouncing into the air,
lost in the stream, you search for
your mask, a bird startled.

Wings sweep your lips,
reveal a word
and a name,
quivering.

Stones

The deepest feeling always shows itself in silence;
not in silence, but restraint
                    — Marianne Moore

Hard and cold, this is your statement.
Pat Lowther tried to warm and shine you,
but was found in the muddy currents

In another country, men use you
to target the "sinners" —
women who dare to expose their faces
or limbs with a free mind.

No eyes to shed tears, no mouths
to tell about the biases, you hold
only harshness, and silence.
Men are satisfied
and clasp together their cold palms
to affirm this "ritual."

But up in the open sky,
some birds fly high and higher;
across the snowcapped mountains,
they see footprints
leading beyond walls;
striking flints
lighting up each torch
to reach out for
shooting stars.

Stranger Moths

after John B. Lee's "The Stranger Moth"

Years ago, you chased away several moths.
Nobody told you
they link to important visitors.

You must have regretted —
too late for your wish
to save them,
and surely you would live
alone and lonely.

Then he told you
for years
you have been the only moth
in his dreams.

Landscape

I want to read your palm
to seek a seasonal landscape.

I long to tie a golden thread
in this labyrinth of dreams
through the winding hall
among fading stars
to your green core.

But I am a fish,
desperate for air.

The air is hot.
You wear your autumn sweater.

In this land,
I shed a summer layer
and swirl in a circle of leaves.

There is a sky above us.
A tree in late autumn.

On departing,
I recall a sudden winter
snow falls.

98

Walking in Rain

A Facebook friend says
sometimes when feeling sad or lonely,
it is easier to talk to a stranger.
You are talking to the heavy rain now,
your shadow dragging in the dim light.

At the conference, the *Star* columnist
shares his tips about walking and writing
— with open eyes and a keen mind
everything around you might be treasure.

The newly arrived book
Two Paths Through the Seasons makes you sad,
as a voice whispers,
one cannot go far or go out,
when one is lost inside.

Spring

I bought a green mat
with the Chinese character "spring."
A black snake in its background
caused my alarm — no safe spot to place it —
the snake hibernated in my dreams.

When I climbed up the top of a hill,
the snake was startled, awake.
I ran to the frozen river and waited.
The ice thawed, my skin was shed —
I saw a beauty in the reflection.

100

My Accent

It is charming.
I assure you,
I assure myself,
and choose to believe so.

Languages have colours.
I want to show you my tender blue.
But you cut off with fork and knife,
quicker than my chopstick taps.

My accent grows trees,
trails and winding roads to
west coast landscape.
It points to the open sky;
yet clouds are too heavy
and form raindrops.

My papers collect them
then dry in silence.
I have hesitated many times
before speaking;
now it develops teeth.

Even with gaps between,
I decide
.......this is my voice.

102

The Lady Oracle

*It is wise not to seek a secret and honest not to
reveal it.*
— *Ben Franklin*

I

You heard her read palms
at a book club.
All palms open,
all books read.

Last night, you dreamt of her —
By the fire, a black cat
sits on her head.
You hide your palms in gloves,
she smiles, "When you are ready…"

But you awake at midnight.
The moonlight runs down on you.
You raise your hands to read
only see them in labyrinths,
and hear a whisper:

The film crew will come
and tell your story with their lines.

The door opens,
I see you...
I see your hurrying feet.
Behind you there's a tunnel
with a life in it.

II

A life in it.
That's what they say.

Yet, in your bed,
you dream of fire and ice.
In your mirror,
a moon wanders in clouds.

Nobody sees
what she sees —
After a storm,
rain puddles wait to dry.
Your horse kicks
the wet ground.
A spider spins
a shining necklace.

In this landscape
tomorrow is distant
and luxurious.

She advises —
forgetting and forgiveness
are twins, wear them both.

Turning inward,
you reach a spring
to drink, a skeleton
to hide.

III

Don't be afraid.
A boat will be provided.

Among hazy fogs
and faceless strangers…
you search.

A church tower casts its shadow,
the black cat dashes out.

106

You open your palms —
no boat, no compass;
only a cracked apple.

They tell dark stories
before and after they come true.
The moon looks back.

lines in italics are from Margaret Atwood's "Another
Visit to the Oracle"

Self Portrait

Dusky coils circle over your head,
blue eggs sparsely seen.
Streams of ants march on your forehead;
your eyebrows shift upward,
sharp like arrows.
Under them deep lakes alert —
light pours in, then bounces out,
splashing stars.
Your nose straightly stands —
two shortened pencils meet up.
Your lips neither in cherry shape
nor with plum flavour,
but birch bark's crack.
Your body, the huge vase
where a tree sprouts up…
Pandora's dilemmas.
A white snake hisses,
then dashes like a shiny sword.
Sirens call,
moon half in clouds —
the canvas folds,
you retreat inside.

The Self-Completing Tree

after Dorothy Livesay

I

No one is surprised;
they call you Emily.
The girl inside you answers.
Yet with hands extending out,
you receive only yourself.

There are walls, still.
There are Emilys, three.
Yet, you are another:
the one who wants to escape a stale life,
the one who could end with broken love.

Listen, you say,
Call us any name you prefer,
but in the end
woman is our name.

Your hands fold on your knees.
Your heart loses its rhythm.
Be a woman...you hear it everywhere
and know that means no name.

II

A tree breaks through the wall,
intruding into your backyard.
You catch a calling from heaven,
the moon face looms.

The tree stretches out,
all branches upward.
You approach this sky ladder,
a shadow following you.

Hesitating, you hear crying
from the underground:
Let go flowery leaves.
Let light shine through.

Removing your belongings,
you see the shadow disappear.
You nod. The tree sways.
Figs fall into your palms.
You spread them out,
wave with your arms:
Now we are free.

110

The Flying Fish

The night you dreamed of the rising river,
a water witch stood in the center.
Through a trembling of ripples
you heard the witch's humming —
rise, rise.

What is the hurry?
You wanted to ask…
only catching a glimpse of
a burning portrait.

You awake to find
a fire glowing inside you.
Over years, you have been
deceived and converted into a flatfish.

The fire flashes,
red wings break through your skin.
Thorns in your eyes, scars on your face,
you soar — an exit, a beginning.

111

Within

after Octavio Paz's A Tree Within

Here I see you
through the thin glass —
the light moves,
you move too.

I come toward you —
to pull you out.
A bird takes off…Bang!
She crashes.

I mourn for her.
The darkness descends.
I lose you.   Both.

Bending down…
A feather lands on my palm;
I see waves, fish…and starry eyes.

The night sky begins to grow
dense feathers.
It draws a tree within…

112

I catch the shape, the sound
and sudden rains...where a pine tree
breaks through the rocky hill of your hometown...
where cherry blossoms rest
on the path you have come along...

I turn off the light...
the flames inside glow.
The tree moves,
I move too.

We move.

113

Contents

Acknowledgments

I would like to thank the editors and judges who originally published the poems listed below in magazines, journals and anthologies:

ARC Poetry: "My Accent" and "Landscape"
Di-vêrsé-city: "Messages"
Rice Paper: "Apples and Pears," "Edge Arts" and "Lorna's Cat"
Red River Review: "10th Anniversary"
EastLit: "Caught"
The Open Heart 9 Poetry Contest: "The Sin City" and "After So Long"
Umbrella: "Snow"
The New York Times: New Year haiku
The Open Heart 8 Poetry Contest: "A House is a Tree," "The Unquiet Bed" and "An Impossible Love"
CBC Radio: "Life Jars"
Window Fishing: The night we caught Beatlemania: "A Glass Onion"

I also want to thank my friend Terry Barker for help and encouragement and my husband Jack Liu and my family for moral support. I am very grateful to George Elliott Clarke and Richard Greene for their interest in my work. Finally, I am very honoured that Marty Gervais and Black Moss Press have accepted this book for publication.